# READ and LEARN

# THE LIFE OF JESUS

by Eva Moore

## Little Shepherd™
### BOOKS

Scholastic Inc.

New York  Toronto  London  Auckland  Sydney

Mexico City  New Delhi  Hong Kong  Buenos Aires

. . . there lived a man named Micah. He was a prophet of the Lord. He spoke out against the kings who no longer obeyed God's commandments. He warned them that the country would be punished because they had led their people from God.

But one day, he said, a great new leader would come to save the people. He said, "Like a shepherd taking care of his sheep, this leader will care for his people by the power of the Lord, his God. The whole earth will know his true greatness because he will bring peace."

Micah said that this peacemaker would rule the whole nation. And he would be born in the small town of Bethlehem.

### Chapter One
## JESUS IS BORN

Mary was like every young girl in Nazareth, a small town in the land of Galilee. Then one day, an angel came to her, and the light of God shone upon her.

The angel said, "Don't be afraid. God is pleased with you, and you will have a son. His name will be Jesus. He will be great and will be called the Son of God Most High."

Mary did not know what to think, but she bowed her head and said, "I am the Lord's servant. Let it happen as you have said."

Galilee was in the north part of Israel (then called Palestine). Most of the people living there were Jews. Other Jews lived in the south, in the land of Judea. The word *Jew* comes from the name of this region, which was called Judah in the Old Testament.

The months passed until at last it was time for Mary's son to be born. One day her husband, Joseph, came to her with unwelcome news.

"We must leave Nazareth," he said. He told her that the emperor Augustus had ordered everyone in the land to go at once to their family's birthplace to be counted for the new taxes. Joseph's family had come from a small town some ninety miles from Nazareth in the land of Judea. It was called Bethlehem.

In those days the country was part of the great Roman Empire that was centered in Rome, Italy. The people in all parts of the Roman Empire had to obey laws that the emperor made and pay taxes to Rome.

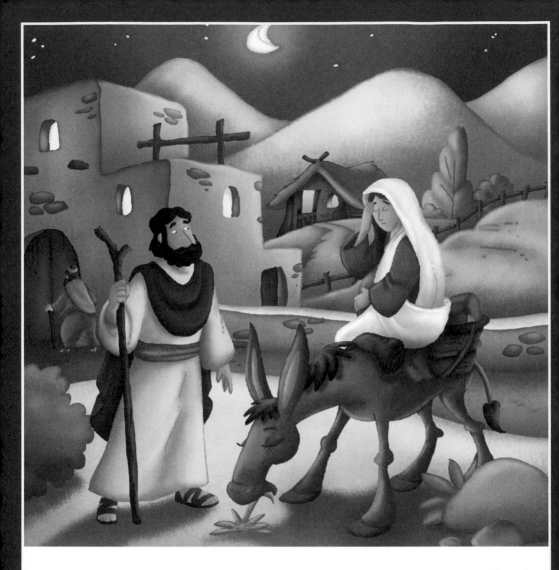

Mary rode on a small donkey while Joseph walked beside her. After three days, Joseph and Mary came to Bethlehem. The little town was very crowded. Joseph looked all over for a room where they could stay. He knew that Mary's baby would come soon.

Finally, a kind innkeeper said they could spend the night in his stable.

Joseph was a descendant of one of Israel's greatest kings, David, who lived one thousand years before Jesus was born. King David was a hero to his people. His birthplace of Bethlehem was also known as "the city of David."

There were cows, goats, and sheep in the stable. There were piles of clean, sweet-smelling hay. The hay and the heat from the animals' bodies made the room warm.

And it came to pass that Mary's baby was born that night.

On the same night, some shepherds were watching their sheep in the fields near Bethlehem.

An angel from the Lord appeared in the sky. The brightness of the Lord's glory shone around them. The shepherds cried out in fear and began to run.

But the angel said, "Don't be afraid! I have good news for you, which will make everyone happy. This very day in the city of David, a Savior was born for you. He is Christ the Lord. You will know who he is because you will find him lying on a bed of hay in a stable."

*Christ* is a Greek word meaning "anointed one," or a person chosen by God to lead God's people. The Hebrew word *Messiah* (savior) has the same meaning.

Suddenly, many angels came down from Heaven. They sang, "Praise God in Heaven! Peace on earth to everyone who pleases God."

The shepherds went to Bethlehem. They found the baby Jesus lying on a bed of hay in a manger. They told Mary and Joseph what the angels had said about their son. Mary thought about this. She wondered what it meant.

## Chapter Two
# THE ESCAPE

Far away, in the East, some wise men saw the bright star. They had never seen it before. They knew that the star meant that somewhere a great leader had been born.

The wise men decided to follow the star and find this special baby. They rode for miles and miles and days and days, always keeping the star in sight. At last they came to the city of Jerusalem, a short distance from Bethlehem. This is where King Herod lived.

These wise men are also called "magi." They studied the stars and believed that when a great leader was about to be born, a new star would appear in the sky.

The wise men went to see the king. They asked him, "Where is the child who was born to be king of the Jews? We saw the star that told of his coming. We have come to worship him."

Another king? No, Herod could not allow that. But he pretended to be glad. He said to the wise men, "The Jewish prophets have said such a leader would be born in Bethlehem. It is close by. Go there and search for the child. If you find him, let me know. I want to go and worship him, too."

Herod the Great ruled over Galilee, Judea, and other parts of the country. He was chosen by the Roman government to look after the people and be sure they paid taxes and obeyed the laws.

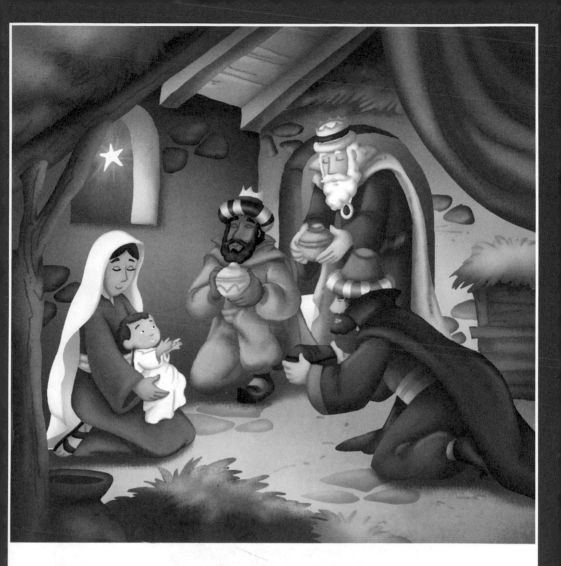

The wise men set out. The star they had been follow-ing led them to Bethlehem.

Here they found the child with Mary. They got down on their knees and worshipped him. They placed before him special gifts for a new king: precious gold and the sweet, strong-smelling spices of frankincense and myrrh.

Later, the wise men had a dream that told them not to go back to Herod. They went home by another road.

Frankincense resin was ground into a powder that could be burned as incense and used in ointments. Myrrh resin was crushed and used in making expensive perfumes and ointments.

17

King Herod was angry when the wise men did not come back. Now he would not be able to find the baby who might one day rule over his land. So he sent for his soldiers. He told them to go to Bethlehem and nearby villages and kill every boy who was two years old or younger.

That night, an angel from the Lord came to Joseph when he was sleeping. The angel told him, "Herod wants to kill your son. Get up! Hurry and take him and his mother to Egypt."

Joseph woke Mary and told her about his dream. They set out for Egypt that very night.

Egypt is where the Jews lived in slavery 1,300 years before. They were led to freedom by Moses. When Jesus was born, there were communities of Jews living freely in Egypt, and they were not under the rule of King Herod.

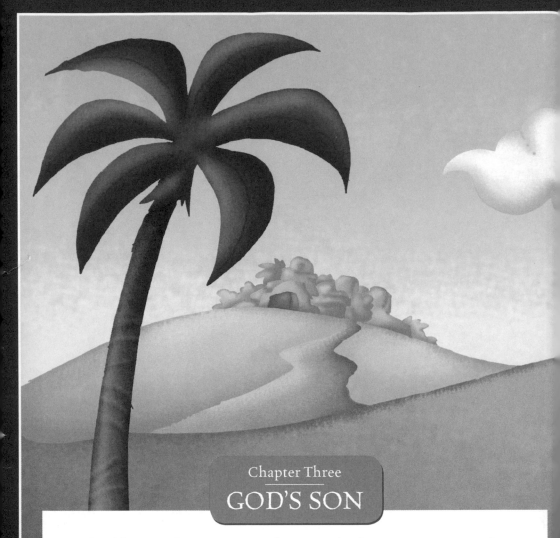

## Chapter Three
# GOD'S SON

In Egypt, Jesus grew from a baby to a young boy. Then King Herod became sick and died. God told Joseph it was safe for him to take the family home to Nazareth.

At home in Nazareth, Jesus played and ate and slept and grew like other children. When he was twelve, Mary and Joseph said he could go with them to Jerusalem for the Passover holiday.

This holiday commemorates the time when Moses led their people out of slavery in Egypt. It lasts seven days (or eight days outside of Israel). It was normal for Jews of Jesus' time to travel to Jerusalem for the holiday if they could.

When the holiday was over, Mary and Joseph left the city and went back home. They thought that Jesus was going back with some other people.

But when they looked for him in Nazareth the next day, they could not find him anywhere. Mary and Joseph made the long trip to Jerusalem again. For three days, they looked for their son. Finally, someone told them that Jesus had been seen in the Temple.

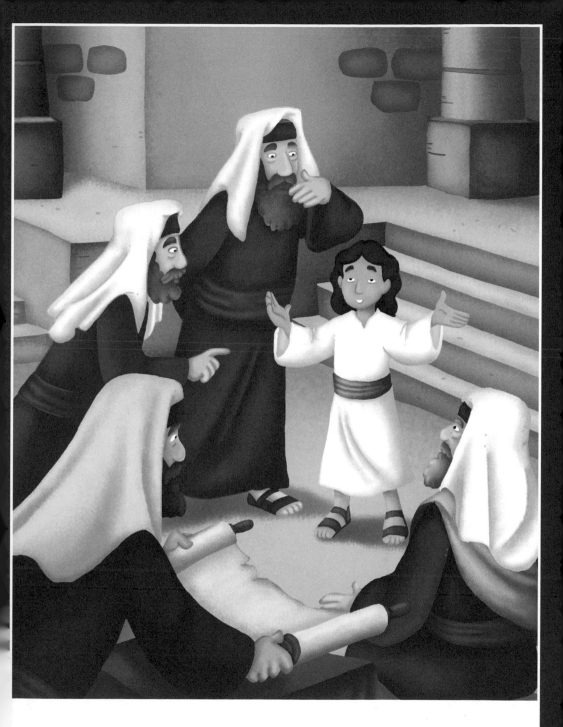

Jesus had been there all along, listening to the learned priests and asking them questions. The priests were surprised at how much the young boy knew.

When his parents saw Jesus, they ran up to him.

"Why have you done this to us?" Mary asked. "We have been so worried. We have been all over Jerusalem trying to find you."

Jesus answered, "Why did you have to look for me? Didn't you know that I would be in my Father's house?"

Jesus was talking about his Father, God, but his parents didn't understand. They were just glad to have Jesus back, safe and sound.

The years passed and Jesus led a quiet life. He stayed in Nazareth and worked as a carpenter, like his father Joseph.

Then, at the age of thirty, Jesus was ready to start the work he had been born to do.

In those days, carpenters were called "cutters" or "workers of wood." They made everything from beams that held up buildings to houses, wheels, cabinets, plows, and other things people used every day.

At that time, a holy man named John was preaching to the people down by the Jordan River. "Turn back to God," John told the people. "Come into the river with me. Your sins will be washed away and you will be forgiven."

Crowds of people came to be baptized in the river.

A person was baptized by being dipped underwater. People who belong to certain churches are still baptized in this way today.

John told people that being baptized was only the first step to leading the kind of life that would please God. He said they must be honest and fair. They must be kind to the poor.

Everyone wondered if John could be the Savior that the ancient prophets such as Micah had spoken of.

But John told them no. "Someone more powerful than I is going to come. I am not good enough even to untie his sandals. I baptize you with water, but he will baptize you with the Holy Spirit."

The Holy Spirit is God's presence at work in the world. Jesus told his disciples that he would send the Holy Spirit to help them and show them what was true.

One day, Jesus the carpenter came to the river. He asked John to baptize him.

After John had baptized Jesus, he knew that Jesus was the true Savior. He did not think he was good enough to baptize such a man. "I ought to be baptized by you," John said.

But Jesus told him this was what God wanted them to do.

Afterwards, Jesus prayed, and the sky opened up. The Holy Spirit came down upon him. It looked like a dove. A voice from Heaven said, "You are My own dear Son, and I am pleased with you."

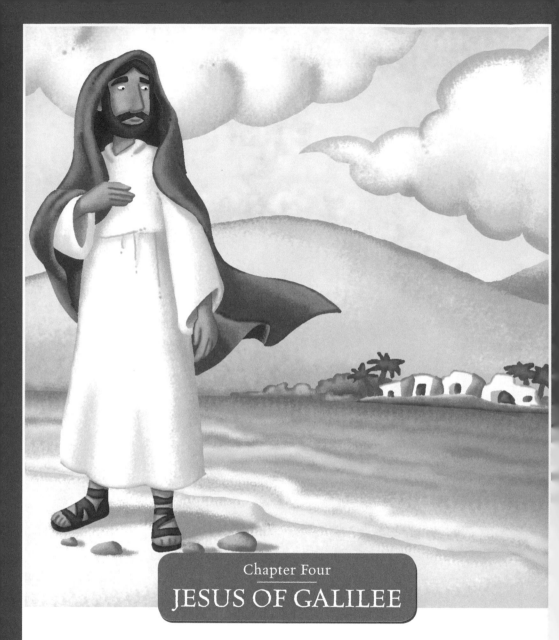

## Chapter Four

# JESUS OF GALILEE

Jesus left Nazareth and went to live in another town in Galilee. It was right on the edge of a large lake. This was where he would begin the work that he had been born to do.

He knew he would need help.

This lake is often called the Sea of Galilee. It is a large body of water, but it does not have salty water and is not nearly as large as a sea. A boat could cross the lake in half an hour.

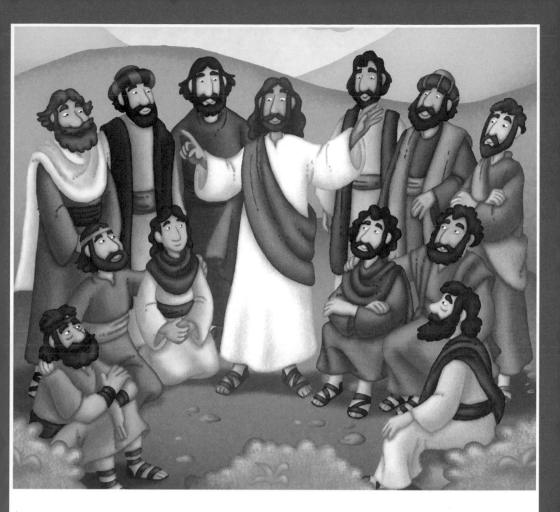

Soon Jesus had found twelve men to be his helpers. They became his special disciples.

The first were two brothers who were fishermen. Their names were Peter and Andrew. Then two other fishermen joined them. They were James and John, sons of a man named Zebedee.

Finally, Jesus chose eight more men to go with him and tell the people about God. Their names were Philip, Bartholomew, Thomas, Matthew, James (son of Alphaeus), Thaddaeus, Simon, and Judas Iscariot.

A disciple is a follower who learns from a teacher. Later, these disciples were also called apostles. Apostles carry on the work of their teacher.

One day Jesus, his mother, Mary, and his disciples went to a wedding in a town called Cana. After a while, the bridegroom became worried. The party was not yet over, but they were running out of wine.

Jesus saw six tall empty jars. He told the servants to fill the jars with water from the well. Then he called for the man in charge and asked him to taste what was in the water jars.

The man was amazed. It was not water at all. It was wine! And it was better wine than they had had before.

So it was in this way that Jesus showed his glory, and his disciples put their faith in him.

John the apostle calls this the first sign or miracle of Jesus.

Later Jesus went to visit a friend. The mother of his friend was sick with a high fever. She felt so bad that she couldn't get out of bed.

Jesus went up to the woman. He told the fever to go away. The next minute, the woman got out of bed. She felt fine. She was able to make and serve them a meal.

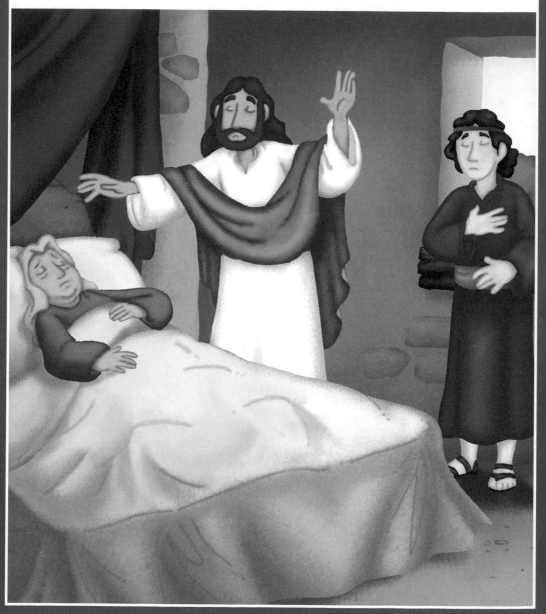

In the evening, people with all kinds of diseases were brought to Jesus. He put his hands on each person. In that second, the person was well again.

The next morning, Jesus got ready to leave the place. But the people gathered around him and asked him to stay.

Jesus said he had to go. "Your neighbors in other towns must also hear the good news about God's kingdom," he said. "That's why I was sent."

More and more people heard about Jesus of Galilee. Soon great crowds came to hear him speak. They came from places nearby and places far away.

Jesus and his twelve disciples went up a mountain. Men, women, and children followed them. Jesus sat on the side of the mountain and the people sat below him.

He told them that God loved them and would bless them if they believed in Him. He told them how to pray and how to please God by being good friends and neighbors. "Treat others as you want them to treat you," he said. "Love your neighbor as you love yourself."

In Jesus' day, teachers sat down when they taught. The people sat down in a semicircle facing the teacher.

## Chapter Five
# MORE MIRACLES

One day, Jesus and his disciples needed to cross the lake. They got into a boat and headed for the other shore.

When they got to the middle of the lake, dark clouds came up and the wind started to blow hard. The waves in the lake splashed up into the boat.

The disciples were afraid the boat was going to sink. Jesus stood up. He told the wind and the waves to be quiet. Then everything was calm.

The other men were amazed. "Who is this?" they asked one another. "Even the wind and the waves obey him!"

When they returned later, people ran to meet the boat. By the time Jesus got to shore, there was a crowd of people waiting for him.

A man broke through the crowd. His name was Jarius. He fell to his knees in front of Jesus.

"Help me," he begged. "My daughter is sick and may die at any minute. Please come and touch her, so she will get well and live."

Jesus went to the house with Jarius. The people inside were crying. They said the girl was already dead.

Jesus said to them, "The child isn't dead. She is just asleep." He went to the girl's bed and took hold of her hand. He said, "Little girl, get up!"

The girl got right up and started walking around. Everyone was surprised.

Then Jesus said, "Give her something to eat."

She ate, and they knew she was not a ghost. She really was alive.

People believed that taking food was proof that a person was alive and well.

While Jesus was in Galilee, he heard some terrible news. The holy man John, who had baptized him in the Jordan River, was dead.

Jesus felt very sad and wanted to be alone. But thousands of people were waiting to hear him speak on a hill nearby. So Jesus and his disciples went to the hill.

Jesus took pity on the people because they were like sheep without a shepherd. He began healing the sick. Then he sat down and began teaching the people about the kingdom of God.

The people stayed all day. The disciples told Jesus, "Everyone is getting hungry. Let them leave so they can go to the villages near here and buy something to eat."

Jesus answered, "They do not need to leave. You give them something to eat."

The disciples looked around to see what food they had. The disciple Andrew came back with a small basket. "A boy gave me these five loaves of bread and two fish. But what good is that with all these people?"

Jesus didn't answer. He turned to the people and told them to sit on the grass in groups of fifty.

When all the people were sitting, Jesus held up the five loaves of bread and two fish. He looked up to Heaven and gave thanks for the food. Then he broke the bread and fish into pieces and gave the basket to his disciples. The disciples took the basket to the first group. The people passed it among themselves and every person had some bread and fish.

The basket went around to everyone. And everyone ate! And when the last group was finished, there was enough left over to fill twelve large baskets.

The news spread all over Galilee. Jesus had fed five thousand men plus thousands of women and children with just five loaves of bread and two fish!

## Chapter Six

# THE GLORY OF JESUS

Later in the day, after all the people had gone, Jesus thought again about John. He told his disciples to leave him for a while. They got on a boat and started back across the lake.

Jesus went up higher on the mountain where he could be alone and pray.

As Jesus was praying, a strong wind started to blow. The wind stirred up the water in the lake. The boat carrying the disciples began to rock back and forth. The men could not row the boat in the strong waves. All night long, they fought to keep the boat from tipping over. They were stuck in the middle of the lake.

A little while before morning, the disciples saw a figure of a man. He looked like he was walking on the enormous waves! He was coming closer to the boat.

The men were terrified and started screaming. They thought the man must be a ghost coming to take them to the bottom of the lake. But then the man said, "Don't worry! I am Jesus. Don't be afraid."

Jesus reached the boat. He got inside. Right away, the wind died down.

Then the disciples worshipped Jesus. They said, "You really are the Son of God."

Jesus knew that God had a special plan for him. Soon his time on earth would be over. One day he told his disciples he would be leaving them shortly. They would carry on his work.

The disciples did not understand. They wondered why Jesus was saying these things.

About a week later, Jesus went up to a mountain to pray. He asked his disciples Peter, John, and James to come with him.

After a while, the three disciples fell asleep. Jesus went on praying. While he was praying, his face changed. It was shining like the sun. His clothes glowed a brilliant white.

Peter and the other two disciples woke up. They saw how glorious Jesus was. And with him they saw the figures of Elijah and Moses, the great prophets from the Bible. They were talking with Jesus about what would happen when Jesus died.

We call this part of the Bible the Old Testament. The Old Testament says that Elijah did not die but was taken to Heaven in a great swirling wind, like a tornado.

Then a voice spoke: "This is My chosen Son," the voice said. "Listen to what he says."

Peter, John, and James were so afraid, they fell flat on the ground and covered their eyes. Jesus touched them and said, "Get up and don't be afraid."

Now Jesus looked the same as he had before. They all began to walk down from the mountain. Jesus told the others he did not want anyone else to know about what had happened. And so they kept it to themselves.

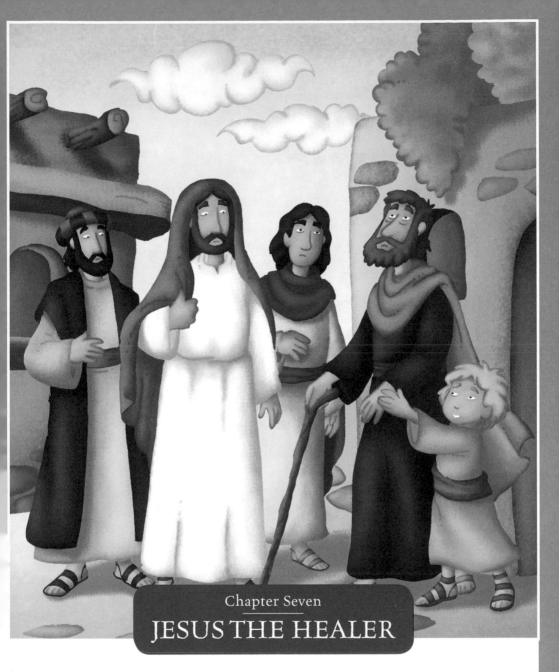

Chapter Seven
# JESUS THE HEALER

One day Jesus and his disciples were walking along a road near Jerusalem. They saw a man who had been blind since he was born. The man had never seen the sun or the moon or the stars. He had never seen his mother and father.

The disciples asked Jesus, "Why was this man born blind? Did he or his parents do something bad that made God punish them?"

Jesus said, "No, they didn't. But because he is blind, you will see God work a miracle for him. As long as I am in the world, I am the light for the world."

Then Jesus spit to wet the ground. He made a ball of mud and rubbed it on the blind man's eyes. He told the man to wash off the mud in Siloam Pool.

The waters in this reservoir inside Jerusalem were believed to have special healing powers.

The man went to the pool and washed his eyes. He rubbed them dry. When he opened his eyes, the man was dazzled by the colors and light. He could see!

People asked him what had happened. He told them that someone named Jesus had come to him and told him what to do.

"Where is this man now?" they asked him.

"I don't know," he answered. "But he must be a prophet like Elijah and Elisha. He could not do this unless he came from God."

Elisha was a friend and follower of Elijah, the Old Testament prophet. Like Elijah, he had special powers. He healed the sick and helped the poor.

Later, Jesus was teaching in a synagogue one Sabbath. He saw a woman who had a bad back. She was crippled and could not stand up straight. She had been that way for eighteen years.

A synagogue is where Jewish people meet to worship God. The Sabbath is the one day of the week set aside to worship God. The Jewish Sabbath is Saturday.

Jesus called her over and said, "You are now well." He placed his hands on her. Right away, she stood up straight. "Praise be to God," she said.

But the man in charge of the synagogue was upset. He told Jesus that no one is allowed to do any work on the Sabbath.

Jesus said, "Don't you untie your donkey and lead it for a drink on the Sabbath? This woman has been tied up with pain for eighteen years. Isn't it just as right for me to set her free on the Sabbath?"

Jesus didn't turn away from anyone who suffered a disease — even the terrible disease called leprosy.

People with this disease had a hard life. They were not allowed to live with their families or come near any person on the street. People who saw them ran away.

But not Jesus. One day he passed the gate to Jerusalem. He saw ten sick men standing along the wall.

One of the men called to him. "Jesus, Master, have pity on us!"

Leprosy is a disease that attacks the skin and nerves; if not treated, the injury to the nerves results in loss of feeling, paralysis, and deformity.

Jesus looked the men in the eyes and told them they were healed. He told them to go and show themselves to the priests.

The men looked at their hands and arms and saw that all of their sores were gone! They ran off.

When people with diseases like leprosy were cured, they had to go to the Temple and show the priests that the disease was gone before they were allowed to go home.

One man turned right around and came back, shouting praises to God. He bowed down at the feet of Jesus and thanked him.

Jesus told the man to stand up. "You may go," he said. "Your faith has made you well."

## Chapter Eight
## TROUBLE IN JERUSALEM

For three years, Jesus and his disciples traveled between Galilee in the north and Judea in the south. Everywhere they went, people came to learn about God.

In one place, some people brought their children to Jesus. They wanted him to place his hands on the children and bless them. But the disciples told the people to go away. They said that Jesus didn't have time for children.

Jesus heard them. He said, "Let the children come to me! Don't try to stop them. People who are like these little children belong to the Kingdom of God. I promise you that you cannot get into God's kingdom unless you accept it the way a child does."

Then Jesus took the children in his arms and blessed them by placing his hands on their heads.

It was springtime. Soon it would be Passover and people from all over the land would be traveling to Jerusalem.

Jesus and his disciples were on their way to the city. They were passing through a village called Bethany. Jesus had friends who lived there, the sisters Mary and Martha. They stopped to see the women.

The sisters invited everyone to have dinner at their house.

After the meal the men got ready to leave. But first Mary had something special for Jesus. She wanted to show him that she loved him and honored him.

Mary brought out a bottle of sweet-smelling perfume. She poured it on Jesus' feet, then wiped his feet with her hair.

The disciple named Judas Iscariot thought this was foolish. "That perfume was worth three hundred silver coins! Why didn't you sell it and give us the money? We could have helped the poor."

It was common for servants in a house to wash the feet of guests. But in doing this herself and using expensive perfume instead of water and her hair instead of a towel, Mary showed special love and respect.

Judas did not really care about the poor. He was just thinking about how good it would be to have three hundred silver coins to add to the moneybag. He was in charge of the moneybag and sometimes he would help himself to a few coins. If there were a lot of coins, no one would notice if he took some.

Jesus replied, "Leave Mary alone. She has done a beautiful thing for me. You can give to the poor whenever you want, but you won't always have me."

When they got near Jerusalem, Jesus sent two of his disciples to the next town to bring back a donkey.

The next day, they entered the city gates. Jesus rode on the donkey and the twelve disciples walked behind him.

People came out to welcome Jesus. They threw palm branches on the road in front of him and shouted, "Hooray! God bless the one who comes in the name of the Lord. God bless the king of Israel!"

Only important visitors were given this kind of welcome. Sometimes clothes were thrown down, too. Today we call this day Palm Sunday.

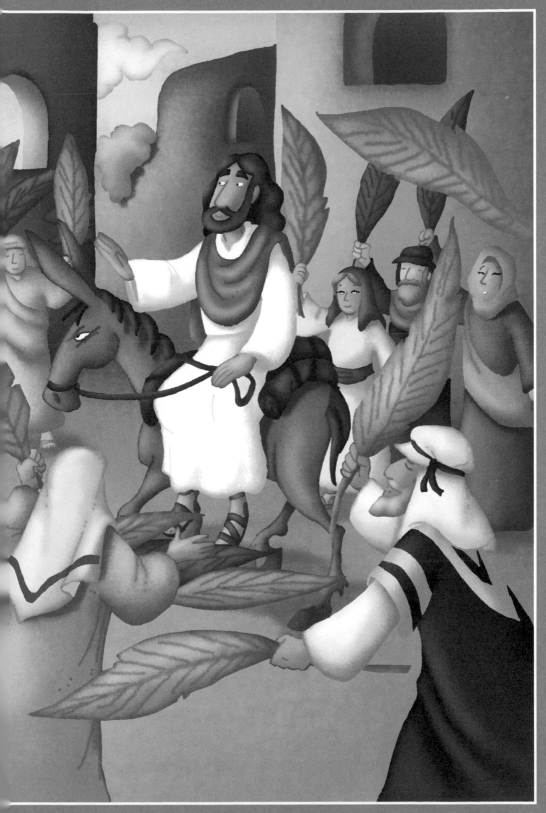

Jesus went to the Temple. He did not like what he saw. The Temple was like a market. People were buying and selling things. There were money changers doing business, trading one kind of money for another.

Money changers would set up tables in the Temple so that people could change their money into the special kind used in religious practice. They were looked down upon because many cheated the people.

The next day, Jesus came back with his disciples. He began to chase out everyone who was buying and selling. He told them the Temple was a place to worship God, not to do business.

This made some leaders of the Temple very angry. For a long time they had thought that Jesus was a trouble-maker. He healed people on the Sabbath. He had people talking about his miracles and the kindness he showed to everyone. They were afraid the people would turn to Jesus and stop listening to them.

These leaders decided they had to get rid of Jesus now, before he got too popular. They got together and made a plan. It all depended on one person.

## Chapter Nine

# THE LAST SUPPER

On the eve of Passover, Jesus and his twelve disciples met in the upper room of a house in Jerusalem. This is where they would have the seder.

Jesus told the others that he would soon be taken away from them. It was time for him to go to God, his Father. Jesus said that after he was gone, they must love one another as he loved them.

This news was terrible to hear. Jesus told his friends, "You are sad now. But later I will see you, and you will be so happy that no one will be able to change the way you feel."

A seder is a dinner in which Jews remember their people's escape from slavery in Egypt (called the Exodus).

Then Jesus said something surprising. "I tell you for certain that one of you will betray me. I will dip this piece of bread in the bowl and give it to the one I am talking about."

Jesus dipped the bread and held it up. Then he moved along the table until he came to Judas Iscariot. He gave Judas the bread.

Jesus means that one of the disciples will turn him over to his enemies.

Judas stood up. He had nothing to say.
Jesus told him, "Go and do what you must do."
The other disciples watched Judas walk away. They did
not know what was going on.

After they ate, Jesus and the eleven disciples went into a garden on the Mount of Olives.

Jesus walked into a grove of olive trees to pray. The others lay down on the ground and went to sleep. They just could not keep their eyes open.

When Jesus came back, he called to his disciples, "Get up! Let's go. The time is here for me to be taken away."

The Mount of Olives is a hill about half a mile east of Jerusalem.

Just then, they heard footsteps. A gang of men with clubs and swords came into the garden.

Judas Iscariot was with them. The others didn't know which one was Jesus. So Judas walked right up to Jesus and said, "Teacher!" And then he kissed him.

The men ran over and grabbed Jesus. They used their swords and clubs to keep the disciples away. They took Jesus down the hill and led him away to be put on trial.

One of the men gave Judas a bag filled with thirty pieces of silver. That was his payment for helping the men catch Jesus.

At this time, it was the custom for men to greet each other with a kiss on the cheek.

In the morning, Jesus was taken before the Roman governor, Pontius Pilate.

Jesus' enemies told the governor, "This man says he is the king of the Jews. He is making people turn against the emperor. He should be put to death!"

Pilate asked Jesus, "What do you have to say for yourself? Are you guilty?"

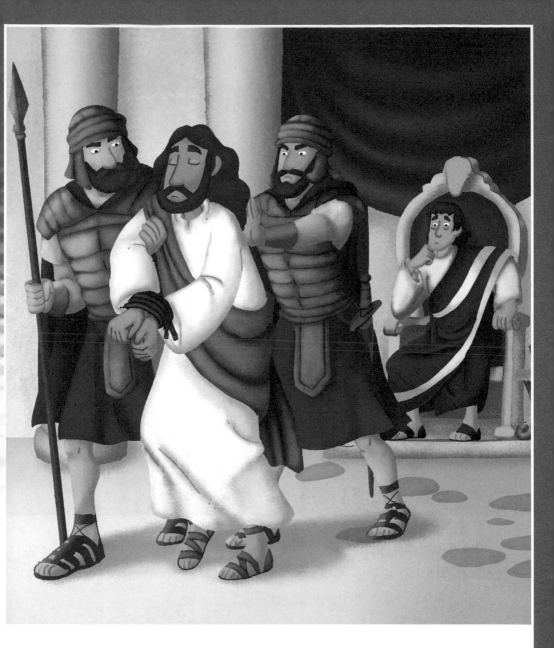

Jesus did not say anything.

The governor was amazed that Jesus did not defend himself. At last, he let his soldiers take Jesus away.

The soldiers put a red robe and a crown of sharp thorns on Jesus. They made fun of this "king." Then they took the robe off and beat him with whips.

They took him to a place called Golgotha. There they nailed him to a cross. This was how the Romans punished people who had committed bad crimes.

At noon, the sky turned dark and stayed that way until three o'clock. At that time, Jesus cried out, "Father, I put myself in Your hands!" Then he died.

A crowd of Jesus' friends was watching everything from a distance. After they had seen the terrible sight, they felt heartbroken and went home.

Golgotha was a spot outside Jerusalem where the Romans carried out executions. In English, it is often called Calvary. Today we call this day Good Friday.

## Chapter Ten

# JESUS LIVES!

One of Jesus' friends, Joseph from the town of Arimathea, came for Jesus' body. He took it down from the cross and wrapped the body in fine cloth. He had it carried to a tomb cut in the side of a rocky cliff. Some women from Galilee were there. They watched Joseph close the tomb with a large round stone.

This is where Jesus' body would rest until they could bury him on Sunday. Then they left to get some sweet-smelling spices to put on his body.

It was the custom to rub oils and spices on a body before the final burial.

On Sunday morning, Joanna, Mary Magdalene, Mary who was the mother of James, and some other women from Galilee went back to the tomb. They were worried that they would not be able to push the stone away from the opening.

To their amazement, the stone had been rolled away. The women went inside. Jesus' body was gone!

Jesus died on a Friday. The next day was Saturday, the Jewish Sabbath. It was against the Jewish law to bury anyone on the Sabbath, so they had to wait until the next day. Today we call this day Easter Sunday.

Suddenly, two men in shining white clothes stood beside them in front of the tomb. The women were afraid and fell to their knees.

One of the men said, "Why are you looking in the place of the dead for someone who is alive? Jesus isn't here. He has risen from death."

The women ran off. They had to tell the eleven disciples right away.

A short time later, two men were walking on the road out of Jerusalem. The men were followers of Jesus. They had believed he was the one who would save Israel. Now they were sad.

Along the way, they met a stranger. The stranger walked with them for a while. He talked with them about everything that had happened to Jesus. The stranger told them not to be sad. Everything had happened as God had planned it.

The stranger went to eat with the men. He picked up a loaf of bread and broke it in pieces. He handed the pieces to the two men. Suddenly, the men knew that the stranger was Jesus. But then Jesus disappeared.

The two men hurried back to Jerusalem. The disciples were all together. They were talking about the news the women had brought. What could have happened to the body of the Master?

They listened to the men's story with great wonder. *Could it be true?* the disciples asked one another.

A little later, the door opened. They saw Jesus before them, just as he had always looked. They could hardly believe their eyes. Then Jesus sat down and ate a meal with them. They knew he was alive.

Jesus stayed with the disciples for forty days. On the last day, someone asked him, "Lord, are you now going to give Israel its own king again?"

Jesus told them they did not need to know what God had planned or when the events would happen.

"But," he said, "the Holy Spirit will come upon you and give you power. Then you will tell everyone about me – people in Jerusalem, in all Judea, and everywhere in the world."

Israel had not had a king since Solomon, David's son, 900 years before. The country had then been split in two and each part had had its own king. Later, the Jewish people had been conquered and their land taken over by other rulers.

After saying this, Jesus got up and went outside. The disciples followed him. Suddenly a cloud appeared over their heads. It covered Jesus and lifted him up into the sky.

The disciples looked up at the cloud. It rose higher and higher. Then it was gone.

They turned to see two men dressed in white clothes standing beside them.

"Jesus has been taken to Heaven," they told the disciples. "One day he will come back in the same way that you have seen him go."

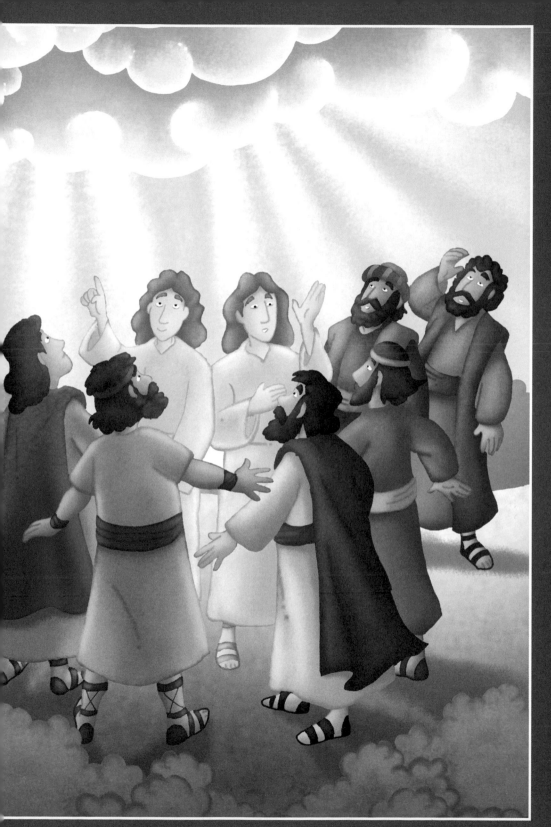

The disciples never saw Jesus on earth again. They carried on his work as he had asked them. His believers grew strong in number so that today, two thousand years later, he lives in the hearts of millions upon millions of people all over the world.

presented to

*Phillip and Rose*

by

*Harley and Joan Clark*

on this date

*1 June 2000*

# BLESS THIS HOUSE

## GLORIA GAITHER

COUNTRYMAN

# FOREWORD

Over a lifetime of traveling, whether driving through cities, small towns, or farm country, I have never gotten over the attraction I have to houses at sundown. When the lights begin to go on and a soft glow washes from the curtained windows, cold architectural structures take on personality. They are not just buildings anymore, they are places someone calls "home."

I can't help wondering about the stories behind the walls. Who lives there? Are they singing? Are they yelling? Is there an awkward silence, or is there deep peace? Is there music playing? Is there a fire blazing in the fireplace? Is someone practicing piano lessons? Frying chicken?

For some of us, the house that shaped our memories was a large, rambling farm house, full of laughter, music, and love. Maybe a big oak table in that picture was the setting for great conversations, hours of homework, and boisterous family dinners.

For some of us, there are houses that hold painful memories of ugly sounds, bad dreams, and hateful words.

For all of us, it is important to sanctify the place we call home—to expel from that space any negative memories and to invite the Spirit of God to sweep it clean, making the rooms sweet and ready for fresh experiences that will foster growth and bring peace.

It is my hope that this blessing will encourage all who would like to sanctify and bless the place we call *home*—whether the home is new or whether you are making a new commitment to make your house a home.

Gloria Gaither

$J$ ust as the builder of this house first

dug deep into the ground

    to pour strong footings on

    which to lay the foundation . . .

    so may you dig deep into the

    soil of God's love to build the

      foundation of your home.

May strong beams of trust, hope, and forgiveness rest firmly on the footings of this love, for it will never be shaken—as mere human love can be—by the storms and weathering of life.

May all the walls be held in place by a sturdy framework of commitment, fidelity, and devotion so that all petitions built from them may be for security and protection . . .

and never walls of estrangement or alienation.

May sunlight fill the spaces and
may moonbeams stream in through
open windows.

May the breezes be allowed to
dance through the rooms
and may the sounds of doves
and songbirds . . . cicadas
and crickets make
happy the hearts that
rest therein.

May no ugly words or violent acts ever enter there to mar or shatter the fragile gift of memory.

$M$ay gratitude, kindness, and encouragement be spoken and demonstrated so often and so naturally in the daily activities of this home that they become the chisel that carves the character and shapes the personalities being formed here.

$M$ay there be music!
May the chords of morning matins
still echo when the evensong
begins,
and may the nights echo their
antiphonal choruses of delight
to the rising sun.

$M$ay this house be a place of celebration because hearts are filled with gratitude for the gift of each new day.

May this family take time to be thankful.

$L$et every "first" be an excuse for
celebration—

the first snowflake of winter,

the first robin in the spring,

the first ripe apple from
the orchard,

the first star at night.

*L*et the children create symbols of
childhood—

      chains of dandelions and
      garlands of daisies,

           snowmen and ice forts,

             mudpies and
             sandcastles.

May the hallways be an art
gallery for fingerpaintings and
construction-paper collages

and the refrigerator a bulletin
board for love notes,
treasured snapshots,
and good report cards.

May the value of this home be measured in sweet memories more than in expensive possessions.

As the years go by, may the dents in the furniture and the nicks in the woodwork become like colorful gems in a filigree setting, provoking precious recollections that, over time, transform mere objects into treasured heirlooms.

When, one by one, the children leave
and rooms grow silent

may the song of life be so
embedded in the walls that it
woos this family to return
for warm reunions,
and causes all who shared this
space to renew old dreams
and realign life's
priorities.

*F*or those who stay, may the warmth of the memories created here be a comfort and a shelter from the fears of the unknown.

❧

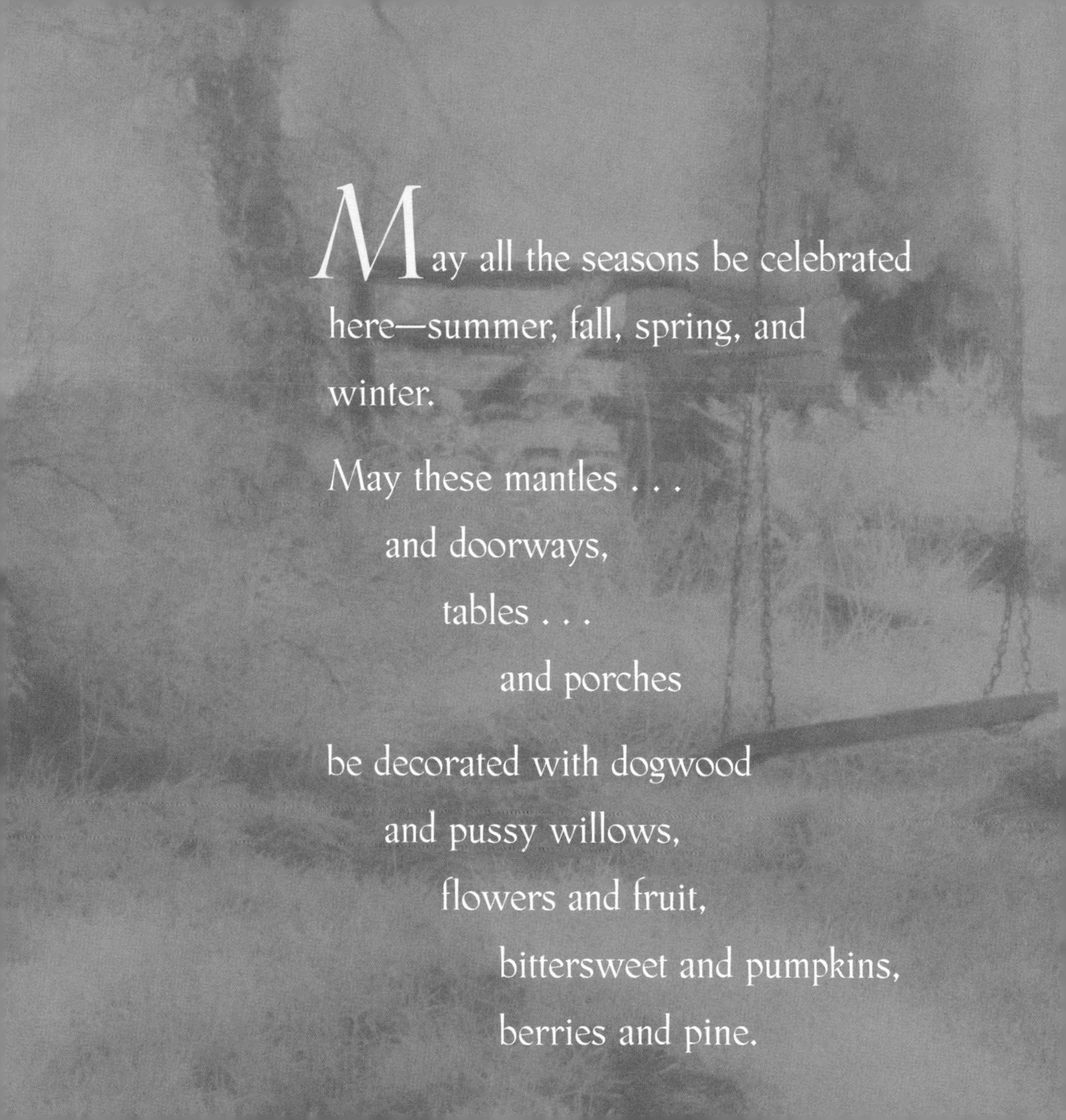

May all the seasons be celebrated
here—summer, fall, spring, and
winter.

May these mantles . . .
    and doorways,
        tables . . .
            and porches

be decorated with dogwood
    and pussy willows,
        flowers and fruit,
            bittersweet and pumpkins,
            berries and pine.

$L$et there be feasting and dancing
. . . laughter and games!

May candlelight flicker . . .
and instruments play . . .
and voices harmonize.

M ay the great Holy days be celebrated here.

May the advent of our Lord be anticipated by sharing the sacred stories of His birth.

Like the shepherds, may those who dwell here hear the singing
of angels in the dull monotony
of routine—
a song that infuses
everything with glory!

May the celebration of the
Resurrection fill each heart
with a sense of joyful victory.

May crocuses and daffodils,
tree buds and green sprouts,
baby chicks and newborn bunnies
all be reminders of the hope of
new beginnings . . .
and may the empty shells
of sunrise-colored Easter eggs
be a happy symbol of an
empty tomb and a risen Lord.

May Saint Valentine's Day teach
those who live together here
to express affection and to find it
natural to say, "I love you."

With fireworks and flags,
bonfires and parades,
may this house celebrate
Independence Day!
May this family exuberantly
express its gratitude
for those who have paid
with their lives
to insure the great
freedoms we enjoy.

$M$ay all who dwell herein give thanks ...

for the bounty of harvest—

for a land so rich and varied—

for a country in which we

may gather freely

to pray and express our

thankfulness to God

"who doeth all things well."

May the sweet aroma of roast
turkey and pumpkin pies,
hot cider and sage dressing
be a memory that will draw all
pilgrims home again and
again to give thanks.
To give thanks!

*L* et there be silence
in this house.

May each child learn to recognize
the gift of silence and embrace it.

May each enjoy the company of
herself or himself as much as the
company of others.

May no guilt or insecurity paint an
ugly picture in any mirror

or raise a cryptic voice to haunt
private thoughts

or taunt high hopes and lofty dreams.

Instead, may silence be a
creative thing

of both energy and peace.

May the wisdom of old age be
respected and valued in this house,
and with the passing of time,
may the generations find delight
in each other's presence.

May the children learn insight and
perspective at their elders' knees—
inspired by wonderful stories of
shared heritage and rich experience.

May each child grow tall,
supported by deep, strong roots
and pulled upward by worthy
aspirations and lofty dreams.

$W$hen sadness or pain or suffering come—as they do to every house—may there be the soothing caress and quick healing of the song of deep joy.

This joy is not the victim of circumstances, but rises from the depths of the soul that knows it is eternal and beyond the reach of earthly cares.

*L*et there be prayer in this house of both praise and supplication.

May prayer be the first and natural impulse when there is
need or plenty . . .
accomplishment or failure . . .
sickness or health . . .
birth or death.

Of all the sweet names of
endearment spoken here . . .
may Jesus be the sweetest
name of all.

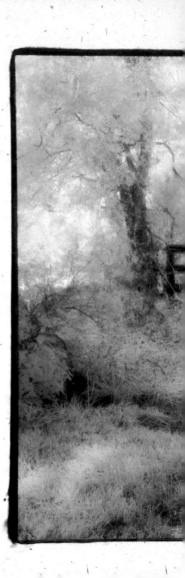

And in this house may all goals,
all resolve, all ambition, and all
aspirations dissolve, at last,
into but one:
          that all who dwell herein catch a
          glimpse of the eternal . . .

and thereafter never be
content until they make their
home forever by the side of Him
who is mother, father,
sister, brother . . .
life, truth, and our eternal home.

May this blessing rest forever
on this house
        and on those who dwell
    herein.

# BLESSINGS ON THIS HOUSE!

Location of house

18208 5TH ROAD        PLYMOUTH, IN 46563

Date we moved in

6 JUNE 2000

Members of family who live here

PHILLIP AND ROSE

Pets who live here

MARVIN (THE CAT)

Our motto for this house

"GONNA LIVE TILL I DIE"